Under Our Feet

poems by

Molly Beth Griffin

Finishing Line Press
Georgetown, Kentucky

Under Our Feet

ACKNOWLEDGMENTS

I'd like to thank my poetry mentors Deborah Keenan, Kathryn Kysar, and
Bao Phi for all their help with this project. I'm also incredibly grateful to
The Loft Literary Center, the Twin Cities writing community (especially my
fellow kid lit creators and my writing group), Hamline University's MFAC
program, and our incredible local bookstores. Sending big love out to all
my mama-friends who get me through my every day and who have been
amazingly supportive of these poems. Both parenting and writing take a
village.

Thank you Emer, Jasper, and Lenore, for making every word of this possible.
You've taught me to see.

Publisher: Leah Maines
Editor: Christen Kincaid
Cover Art: Emer Griffin
Author Photo: Bao Phi
Cover Design: Elizabeth Maines McCleavy

Printed in the USA on acid free paper.
Order online: www.finishinglinepress.com
also available on amazon.com

Author inquiries and mail orders:
Finishing Line Press
P. O. Box 1626
Georgetown, Kentucky 40324
U. S. A.

Table of Contents

April Snow

Spring turns
and looks back at winter
with all the indecision
of becoming.

Dark clouds loom outside our west
windows, sun streams in from the east—
I look east—and dress the kids
for the wrong season.

Flakes fly in April,
cling to green grass,
and every year
we are surprised,
as if snow was a betrayal
even though it never sticks.

By now we should know
nothing moves forward without
hesitation, there is no change
without doubt,
but in time, the wrong season
will always become
the right one.

Monday Morning

A sharp-shinned hawk
perched on the fence in our backyard
hunting sparrows or mice.
I rushed to get my son,
but the hawk glided down the alley
with a swoop of gray wings
and barred tail.

Later,
on the walk to the bus stop
he spotted two robins
hopping through the grass
of our neighbor's yard.
His wild body slowed,
and he followed them carefully,
quietly, at a distance.

When they finally flew off,
he said "I can't believe there were *two of them*.
I can't believe they were *right there*.
I can't believe I spotted them *first*."

I said, "You don't miss a thing, do you?"
A lot of the time he sees
much more than I do.

Balance Bike

She plants her feet on either side
of the frame
and walks, slowly.

The wheels turn, slowly.

The sidewalk inches past, slowly.

Every now and then she bends
down
to watch an ant.

And then she hobbles on.

She somehow thinks this is fun,
even though she would go faster
without the bike beneath her.

I wait for the moment when she discovers
the glide,
when she figures out how to push
off, and lift her feet
and sail down the sidewalk,
the world rushing past
in a blur.

But I also cling to these steady plodding steps
—this snail's
speed
at which
she moves away from me.

Contained

Last night we found the empty shells
of cicadas clinging to the warm retaining walls.
We gently pried them off and held them,
light and brittle on our palms, to look closer.

These creatures waited 17 years as nymphs,
burrowing in darkness beneath the ground.
Finally they tunneled out into the bright glare
of summer, and shed their too-small skins.

I've lived twice that long now, and I wonder
what it would feel like to unzip an old self,
climb out, and be reborn—bigger, brighter—
with an urgent song to sing
and a hollow belly to amplify it.

Amateur

My mother bought me a camera for Christmas,
a much nicer one than I could afford.
It's automatic, but still, I'm learning its knobs
and buttons, the long barrel of its lenses
and the way they twist in my hands
to bring the world closer, move it farther
away, draw it into sharper focus, blur
its edges out. I'm not used to this level
of control.

It's large and heavy, and I only get it out
for special occasions, like this trip
to the north shore of Lake Superior, times when
I know there will be much beauty and also
enough adults—another bag won't be a burden.

I snap a hundred photos, and I think,
yes this—the way my daughter's hair falls
across her cheek when she looks for rocks.
Yes this—the silhouette of my son climbing
long-legged, against a distant horizon.
And these clouds, and these waves, and also
these smile lines around my mother's eyes
while she watches them play.

Of course part of me wants the pictures
to be good, but mostly I don't care.
I am an amateur. One who loves.
It has become a way of paying attention.
A way of saying yes, and thank you
when so much of motherhood has been
saying no, no, not this again, I can't.

Today I take a hundred pictures
to say thank you for this perfect moment,
and this one, this beautiful thing,
and this one. I never thought
there'd be so many moments
I'd want to keep.

Believe

There's a splatter of blood in the sink
and a hole where a baby tooth
used to be, but the tooth itself
isn't just lost—
it's missing.

I assure him the Tooth Fairy will come anyway,
but by bedtime he gets me to admit
that the Tooth Fairy is pretend.
I say something like what I say about Santa:
that it's a story, a good story,
and he can decide if he wants to believe it.

He doesn't want to believe in anything
that isn't strictly speaking true
(fossil-record true,
food-web true,
weather-pattern true)
but he'd like money under his pillow anyway.

After his light is out,
I wish I'd said something better about stories
and the power of believing things
unproven.

I know his kind of awe
is reserved for facts.
But there are some things,
like the importance of a baby tooth
(here, and then gone)
that we can both believe in.

Underneath

Garish beauty bursts all around— first blooms
and buds and brightness—
but there is a different kind of beauty we unearth
while clearing out the garden beds.
Darker and more subtle; fragile and precious.

Look: a tiny bird's skull,
it's curves brittle and delicate.

Look: a stripped stick,
covered in eaten-away patterns.

With feathers rotted away, bark gone,
what's underneath is revealed.
It is laid out here—bare—on our kitchen table
for us to study with magnifying glass and camera,
with one outstretched finger, trembling.

They are miraculous here—bare—
but what is more miraculous still
is the notion that each of the birds out there,
feathered and flapping,
has this sculpted perfection beneath the surface,
That twigs, still bark-covered and tree-bound,
can hide an intricate pointillism inside.

One Definition of Privilege

In college
I could analyze texts in Spanish,
and write essays in Spanish,
and critique art in Spanish.
This morning, twelve years later,
I could not understand
the kids at the bus stop
speaking Spanish to their mom.

This morning I smiled at her,
the other mom, looping backpack straps
around one child, zipping the raincoat of the other.
I smiled, and nodded hello as I always do,
but silently, because I do not trust my ears,
or my tongue, not to mangle her language.
I am allowed to keep my ignorance
to myself.

Once I invited her into my car when it was thirty below,
and we waited together for the afternoon bus.
We exchanged a few words in English,
and I learned her name is Antonia (Tonia, for short).

She wrapped her mouth around my language,
and made me understand, but I was (I am) embarrassed
to show her my rusty college Spanish
that doesn't even know the word for lunch box
or the word for ashamed.

Tummy

She burrows under my shirt
and rests the curve of her small cheek against my belly.
"I love your tummy so much," she says. "It's so warm."
Since she weaned, my belly has become her comfort
object: when she is sad, or tired, or lonely, or hurt,
she pulls my clothes aside and folds herself against
my middle. Pats it. Squeezes it. Kisses it.

She tries to teach me. But still, I see myself in pieces:
soft parts and strong parts and parts creased by years
and parts stretched by experience. The silver is slowly
taking over the dark of my hair, the way I find raspberry
canes sprouting up in the lawn. And I try not to turn
from the mirror, hide from the camera, shy away
from her hands pulling my clothes aside
and her arms stretching around as much of me
as she can reach and saying, "I love this so much."

Claiming Our Prince

Purple rain fell the day that Prince died
and everyone in Minneapolis had a story to tell.
My story was simple.
I wasn't a big fan, but I grew up
practically next door to his estate.
When I was a kid we joked
that we should bring over a pan of brownies
and introduce ourselves, but we never did.
There were gates and fences,
though I'm not sure that was why
we stayed away.

I listened to other peoples' stories
and learned that he was a strange
kid who got beat up in the halls,
but of course he went on to make art,
connect people, and change the world.

When he died, fans wove
purple yarn though his fence, tied
balloons to the gate. The whole city
danced, mourned, claimed him again
and again. In all this, his strangeness
was not forgotten. If anything,
it was celebrated.

The next day my first grader
tried to learn multiplication
at the breakfast table,
even though he still struggled to open
the toothpaste himself or decipher
the rules of conversation
to make a friend.

And I thought: maybe there is hope
for this strange kid, too.
Maybe someday he will be celebrated.
Maybe the world is changing,
or at least becoming a place where neighbors
look beyond strangeness, cross fences,
bring brownies, and introduce themselves.
Let's open the gate, talk about the weather,
tell a story, and claim each other
again and again.

Weight

So many women walk into the gym
with weight they want to lose.
It's like they carry it in their hands
and hope to set it down someplace
and forget it there;
it's like they hope
that it doesn't really belong
to them after all.

But the weight
of wanting to be less
is heavier than thighs
or butts or bellies.

No, in here, in this gym,
these women want to be more.
They pile their plates high,
stacking weights
onto their bars
and asking their bodies
to lift, and sweat,
asking their bodies
to build, and grow—

because what do we gain
by losing
ourselves?

These women grunt and growl,
and teach me to push my body
for more, to take up space
and not walk out of here
with less
than all of myself,

because it all belongs
to me.

Rules in a Storm

We walk to the bus stop in the pouring rain,
and I try to explain to you that the rules
are different in a storm.

Yes, we can wait for the school bus on our neighbors' porch,
even if we do not know them. No, they will not mind.
I promise you the driver will wait, with the bus's yellow arm
beckoning, while you run across the street.
Yes, your teacher will help you strip your boots
and raincoat off, and tie your sneakers on.

In a storm, everyone is more willing to wait,
to help, to give each other the benefit of the doubt.

One time I picked up three soaked runners
who huddled against tree trunks by the lake.
Yes, I waved three large half-dressed men
into my backseat, and drove them to their cars.
No, I would never do that, except in a storm.

You skip over puddles, and climb into the warm belly
of the bus. I watch you, and wonder
if we could always be more generous and patient
with children whose differences are invisible,
with strangers who carry their storms inside.

Things that Fall in the Night

The night we dropped bombs
on Syria
my children both needed baths.
They cried over water drops
in their eyes
and other silly little things.
(Apples for snack.)
(The wrong pajamas.)
And when I finally had them tucked
into bed, when they'd finally fallen
asleep, I saw on my phone that the
bombs
had fallen sometime in there,
between bath
and bedtime.

I sat on my couch, looked
at maps, read
about regimes and intervention
and pacifism and refugees.
No easy answers except
nothing that fits
between bath
and bedtime
should be this big.

I know it doesn't fit.
It is huge and complex.
And yet, this single action—
this yes, this go— this happened
tonight. The bombs
fell
while I was rinsing shampoo
from a small head
and a child's tears
came down.

Translucent

As we walk through the neighborhood, my son
tries to explain to me why tulips are so pretty.
"It has to do with how the sun comes
through them. Especially the red ones."

He's using the word *reflection*,
but he knows that's not really right,
and so we talk about what *translucent*
means. And then he crouches down, low
and close, and tells me that where the petals
overlap, they're darker, and so we talk
about *opaque*.

This discussion of color and light and beauty
lasts the whole way home. I say,
"I love that you're good at noticing
pretty things. You've always been good
at that. At paying attention."

When he's paying attention,
I see the beauty move through him,
and I wish we could all be kaleidoscopes
for each other.

The Work of Small Creatures

These tight, round peony buds
make a nectar that's irresistible
to ants, and so the ants crawl around
and through them, around and through
them, bodies glowing gold
in the evening sun.

Some say the ants help work
those dense buds loose
and help the giant flowers open.
Some say the flowers can open
just fine on their own.

I think that most big beautiful things
rely on the hard work of small creatures
that usually go unnoticed, or even
dismissed, and so I decide
to say thank you just in case.

How to Spell 'Realize'

He's writing a long book about dinosaurs fighting—
each letter small and careful, each predator/prey
relationship researched for plausibility.
He's dutifully copied out the jumbled
consonants of their tongue-twister names,
but he comes bounding in every few minutes
to ask me how to spell some important word
for the story, some tricky word
like 'neither,' or 'realize,' or 'surrounded.'

He is amazed that I know so many words
and the way their letters fit together like puzzles
in my head, but he's distraught when I ask
if he means 'since' or 'sense,' 'where' or 'wear,'
can he use it in a sentence
so I know which one to spell?

He doesn't like ambiguity. He believes
in right and wrong, that the world should follow
rules, like a dinosaur from the Triassic
can't eat a dinosaur from the Cretaceous.

But language has more exceptions than rules,
and yes 'realize' has an 'a' in it, as if the word 'real'
lives right there inside, even though your mouth
doesn't quite get around to saying it.

As his dinosaur drama marches forward,
graphite on printer paper, I want to tell him that it's worth
bending your mind around language that won't behave,
because this is just the beginning of what, one day,
you'll be able to do with words.

One day, when you write a misbehaving word
like 'realize' on the page, it will make something real
happen. It will put some puzzle together
in your mind, and make your mind
misbehave too.

Post Office Starscape

Sometimes,
in the late afternoon
when you've come to buy stamps,
the sun shines through gaps
in the patterned brick wall
and makes a grid of light
on the concrete building.

Sometimes,
it looks like a disco ball
has frozen mid-spin,
or some constellations
were stolen
from the planetarium
and projected here.

Sometimes,
something plain
and unremarkable,
is made beautiful
by a pattern of bricks
and an angle of light,

but only
if you happen to be here
at the right moment,
and only if you stop,
and look.

On Water

This teaspoon-sized duckling
is distracted and separates
from the zigzag swarm
of peeping brothers and sisters
paddling obediently
around their mother.

It swims so fast to catch up
that the swimming
becomes running
on the pond's surface.

It is a miraculous mistake
of lightness, and smallness,
and urgency,

and the wrenching anxiety—
that pang of fear
at being left behind—suddenly
becomes elation.

For a moment,
inside that tiny chest,
a tiny heart
hammers the rhythm:

I can,
I can,
I can.

Night Heron

It's been a wet summer
of soggy basements and leaky roofs,
and there is a soccer field beside the road
on my way to the grocery store
that has flooded into a semblance of a pond.
In this shallow water, a stocky figure wades:
a night heron, smoky gray and white
and crested with dark feathers.
She doesn't know that this isn't a real pond
or doesn't care.
There can't be fish here,
but frogs and bugs are just fine with her.
She is an opportunist.

I drive past wondering
if today is a perfect writing day
or if today is the day,
so long after childbirth,
when I should start
to knit my body back together.
She shoots her dark eye my way
across the rippling water,
like she's saying,
"A bird that waits for perfection,
goes hungry."

Robin's Egg Blue
(for Orlando)

I am so angry about the 49 people dead
in Orlando, shot for dancing,
for loving, for being themselves,
that I nearly step on it:
the half egg shell on the sidewalk,
tiny, perfect, abandoned.

What kind of bird hatched from here?
The obvious startles me—we probably call
this color *robin's egg blue* for a reason.

I cup it carefully in my palm,
thinking of fragility, and strength,
and the somewhere-robin that has outgrown
this brittle curve of sky,
cast it off, left it here for me to find.

I walk home marveling
at how words can live inside us
unclaimed—
words like *pride*,
and *Pulse*,
and *robin's egg blue*—
long before experience
demonstrates their truth,
long before that truth hatches,
wet and wobbly,
under a bigger sky.

Weeds

I wait for you to pick me up,
and as I sit on my front steps,
I idly pull a clump of matted grass
from a crack in the sidewalk.
Before I know it I'm weeding
all up and down the front walk,
killing five minutes or ten
before you pull up to the curb,
letting the little piles grow
around me, even though
I don't have gloves on, even though
there won't be time to clean up after,
even though I'm in work clothes.

I rip out leaves and scraggly roots
and sandy soil, and I think maybe
in the car, you will see the dirt
beneath my nails and you will think
I'm *That Kind* of person,
instead of just someone who is embarrassed
by her out-of-control yard.
And maybe you will smell this work on my skin,
this green smell, this sweat smell, this sunshine
smell, and think I am some kind of earth mother
instead of just someone whose whole life
has weeds growing out of the cracks.

The Baby Tapir

I'm potty training my daughter and we're both worn out,
so I put her in a diaper and take her to the zoo.
I need a break from cleaning up pee; she needs a break
from trying to be big.

Later, back home and on the potty again,
we're talking about what we saw at the zoo
and we laugh about the silly baby monkeys.
Then she says she loves the stripy baby tapir—
where was the stripy baby tapir today?
"We saw the baby tapir," I remind her, "it just isn't stripy
anymore. They only have stripes for a little while."
She looks at me, and she bursts into tears.

I get her off the potty and I hold her, and she slips
her hand under the collar of my shirt to comfort herself.
She cries and cries, a sobbing child in Wonder Woman
undies. She cries and cries, because the baby tapir
doesn't stay stripy, because being little doesn't last.

To Witness

Tonight,
everybody walked outside
to sit among the crickets
and watch the lunar eclipse.

Tonight,
the screen doors banged shut
behind a hundred thousand
people, a million people,
a hundred million people
stopping everything
and looking up.

Tonight
was a one-woman show
with an audience spanning continents.
She took the stage and said stop.
You are lucky to see this.
You are lucky that the rain
is holding off till morning.

Broken

(for Philando Castile, and all the others)

I've got a brake light out on my car.
It's been out for weeks, and I keep saying I need
to get that fixed, but I don't, because I need
to take care of too many other broken
things. My house is a mess and my kids need
dentist appointments and yes, I also don't fix
it because I know that I won't get pulled over
for something like that, something so small,
and if I did, the cop whose salary I pay to serve
and protect me wouldn't even write me a ticket.
He'd say, "Get that fixed, honey. Drive safe."
And I'd cringe at his tone, but I'd drive away, safe.

I don't know when I'll die, or how,
if it will be by disease or accident,
but do I know that I won't die
at the hands of a police officer
on the street in the night beside my car,
with my hands up and my children watching,
all because my brake light is broken,
it isn't flashing red and saying *stop,*
please stop, don't you know this world
is broken enough?

The Snow Whale

Late for the bus, as usual,
I coax my son along
step by step by molasses-slow step.
I try to stay patient, try to make it a game,
try to feign jolliness.

Just as I'm starting to lose it with him,
he says "Mama, a WHALE!"
He plops down on his knees on the sidewalk.
I tip my head back and try to take a deep breath,
but the air hurts my nose, my throat, my lungs.

Every day we do this, I think. *Every day.*
And I am so exhausted, and cold, and late.

But then I look down and sure enough,
there *is* a whale. Not just a whale,
a humpback whale, with a pectoral fin and tail flukes
and an eye just exactly where an eye should be.
"Did somebody make it?" he asks, in awe.
"I don't think so," I say.
"Did it fall from the sky?"
"I don't think so."
And I try to explain that it was made by chance,
maybe from a footprint or a snowball,
maybe just from a slice of snow
that somebody's shovel missed.
But really I don't know. "I guess it's a miracle,"
I say, "because we needed a whale today."

Sometimes
we find exactly what we need
under our feet.

Molly Beth Griffin is the author of the young adult novel *Silhouette of a Sparrow* (Milkweed Editions, 2012) and the picture books *Loon Baby* (Houghton Mifflin, 2011) and *Rhoda's Rock Hunt* (Minnesota Historical Society Press, 2014). Her novel was featured on the ALA Rainbow List and the Amelia Bloomer List of Feminist Literature, was a Foreword Book of the Year, and received the Milkweed Prize for Children's Literature. Her picture books have won a Jeanette Fair Book Award, a NE Minnesota Book Award, and a Star of the North nomination. Her writing has also been awarded two Minnesota Arts Board grants, and a McKnight Fellowship. Molly is a graduate of Hamline University's MFA program in Writing for Children and Young Adults, and a teaching artist at The Loft Literary Center. She lives in South Minneapolis with her partner and their two children.

www.ingramcontent.com/pod-product-compliance
Lightning Source LLC
LaVergne TN
LVHW021126080426
835510LV00021B/3341